THE QUEEN

A POEM

Also by Dorothy Baker

Picking Up Gum Wrappers & Everyday Magic

THE QUEEN

A Poem

DOROTHY BAKER

TSP

TRAVELING SHOES PRESS
PO BOX 332
Pioneertown, CA 92268

The Queen
ISBN# 978-1-732-92055-2

Second Edition | 2020
Book design by Jon Christopher

INTRODUCTION

The Queen would like me to introduce her. Well, here goes. She is from the twelfth century: however time means nothing to her. She enjoys twenty-first century amenities. Her heart is resolute that war is obsolete. She goes about her days like the free spirit she is.

As the writer of these ditties, I discovered her one day when she helped me put down in words the opening poem about earrings. It gave me a giggle and I wondered who she was and what else she had to say. I read this first poem to an author friend (who was reading the Wall Street Journal and having his breakfast coffee on the back deck.) His response was "That took courage." That did it, I was caught in the space of framing my thoughts through a 12th century perspective and The QUEEN began to speak.

I like to play around with rhyme. Poets have carte blanch anymore to follow no rules. The disciplines of old are no more. The little book, The Queen, is an example.

Dorothy Baker
February 14, 2020

THE QUEEN

A POEM

I.

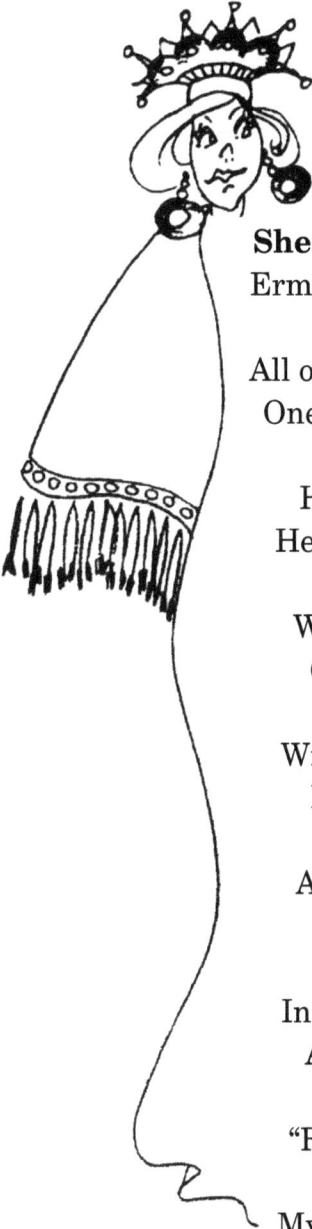

She dressed quite simply
Ermine tails, red fingernails

All of the trappings befitting
One of her sitting… in life.

How did she measure
Her subjects' displeasure

When seeing her sport
(Alas, even in court)

Without any tears… her
Newly pierced ears?

At last she could wear
Her grandest pair.

In the hall she appeared
And everyone jeered.

"Rats," cried the Queen
"What do you mean
My earrings are too big?"

II

She goes to school
She's no fool

The more one knows
The prettier one's toes

Or so she'd heard said
(I don't know who
She's listening to.

Do you?)

As she passed by the royal maids
She was handed her semester grades

What... an F in drawing?
Well, perhaps in sawing

You must be mistaken
This class I have taken
Ten times now at least
Just ask the Priest

He'll tell you what's so
For I have to go

The Chancellor awaits his Queen.

III.

"Ten minutes to ten
Where are my kin?

They are scheduled to meet me
In the garden to treat me

It's my birthday, you know.

Eh, they like to sleep in,"
She said with a grin

"They'll be here soon
I'll just take this spoon

And taste the plumcakes
The cook always bakes

Oh, a bit sour it seems
Just like my dreams."

She worried all night
That her clan just might

Forget altogether
And leave her no tether

To rein in her fame
As the glorious dame

And Queen of this magnificent land.

IV.

Her majesty is always late
Not something one can arbitrate

Her sense of time is lacking
Her sails set wrong for tacking

The Royal yacht missed the port
While the pages waited to escort
The tardy queen

Fire the rascals who make the clocks
Then the brigands who tend the locks

But get her barge
A mite too large

Past all the lights that guard the slip
Into the cove for her nightly dip

She takes to the water in the altogether
Her robes she tosses in any weather

The Queen, it seems, calls all the shots
"I don't care if the kingdom rots
I'll have my swim."

V.

Once every month at least
Until her menses ceased

She would charter a carriage
And consider a marriage

To the Prince of Holly Berry.
He was short and fat
No matter about that

His fortune complete with land
His shores replete with sand

All that she treasures would be
Hers… eventually

And then some hussy
Whose hair was fuzzy
(A cousin, no doubt)
Gave her the rout

Tumbling her apple cart
She didn't feel so smart

Retreating… as it were
Into her ermine fur

She ordered her carriage
Turned round to disparage

A prince who was fickle
Who chose a Popsicle
Not nearly the Queen's station in life.

VI.

On sale she always buys
Being very wise
And Queen to boot.

It was such fun
To make a run
Cloaked as a merchant
To be sure.

Everyone knew, of course
She couldn't even
Fool the horse,

But they all pretended
Not one intended
To disclose

Where the Queen
Was buying her clothes.

If she fancied a hat
That was that
She would have it.

What gave her away
I'm here to say
Was this exotic couture
Though she was demure

Her tailor would soften the blow
Keeping her in tow
By emptying her bag
Before she could buy
Just one more new rag.

VII.

Was it her chat
Perchance her hat

That
Sent them all fleeing?

Would she ever be sure
Of a possible cure?

At the court she would try
Their attention to pry

From the hapless rendition
Of the country's condition

Or

Who toppled the boat
And fell in the moat?

It was the Queen's daily task
But surely if you had to ask

The Queen rarely wanted to rat
And on top of that

She was the one who would flee.

VIII.

She liked to stow her crown
And amble into town

A hamlet half the size
To the Queen's royal surprise
Of what she'd been told.

Her subjects went to and fro
Just as she was wont to go.

In slippers of silk
They would guess her ilk

So she traded the guard
His boots for the yard

Laced them up tight
So she could look for her knight
To come riding by.

He hasn't shown yet
But you can bet

The Queen continues to spy.

IX.

Ideas float around her head
Even when she's in bed.

"So exciting," she remarked
Then on the trail she embarked.

Where it would lead
She had no need to know.

If you think she's content
That's not what I meant.

The Queen's new reasoning
If you can call it that

Needs some seasoning
To bring it to bat.

The Queen knows full well
That no one can tell

At this moment in time
If her life is a rhyme

Or a series of misses
Of hugs and kisses

And mysteries of every kind.

X.

She took up writing
It was so exciting
Just a pen and a journal.

Where was the Colonel
To stop this pursuit?

She had turned on the mute
And silenced her courtier's advice
Which wasn't very nice

But, then
She was the Queen.

Poems poured from every cranny
Of her brain
Some she would disdain
Yet it was very plain

She was having a blast
This Queen.

Her life is a chasm to mine,
Her work to dredge
Beyond the hedge
And dig up the parts sublime

What a pity
She's in a city
But perhaps that
Will even be better

She said so in her letter,
To me,
This Queen of reality.

Tucked into the folds
Of her Ermine robes
A life of wit
Of sweat and spit
Just like any other.

I'll wager you'd agree
This Queen of words is free
To be who she is.

XI.

The margins of her papyrus
Leave no space
Words fill every trace.

She's very committed
And early down-sitted
Each morning to write.

Aggressively slow
Her sometimes foe
Came sauntering in

Because of his pace
She could quickly erase

Any hoe he could throw
In the hallowed flow
Of her morning rites.

First though let's see
Her meditation free
Is where it all starts.

At this point in time
She will often climb
To the heights of oneness needed.

The Queen's morning
Finished

Her upper arms warm
From the rush

Of hearing her words
The rills and the terds

Of poetry's constant remand
And demand
To be **heard.**

XII.

I thought she was my friend

But when the king died
All she could do

Was cling fast to her dog
And hug and hug her dog.

When she leaves the chamber
It's goodbye pal, there, there

Here's your water
I've left on the air.

While I
Stand by

The Queen on high
With no salutation.

She sobbed for days
At her horse's passing
With just a stare for me.

Truly rare
When she gives a care for another.

If their purse were deep
She might then weep.

I thought she was my friend.

XIII.

"Woe is me," said she
"I haven't drunk my tea."

"Too many presented at court
Too many ladies in waiting
Too many messages to send
Too many hooks to be baiting
Just too much to do."

"My hair needs henna
My nails need polish
My cousin is coming at three."

They had planned an adventure
Just the two of them.

When you are Queen
Lest you be seen in the country
You must pull the shades down
In your coach

Which found the kin at odds within
Over where to go
Since they couldn't show… their faces.

In the tiny cab bumping knees
They found it hard to please… one another.

"Shall we just… get out here
And open the beer?"
Asked the cousin.
The Queen agreed and stopped the steed.

Disembarking she found
Her veil turned around

Which was against the law
But, hey, she was the Queen
What does the law mean… to her.

They enjoyed their repast
Ope'ning the beer at last

Remembering the day
The Queen would say,

"Beer tastes better than tea."

XIV.

Who is she? They whispered
As she crossed the moat
Disguised, this time, riding a goat.

Her plans vague
The first leg
Of her journey not plotted,
'Till just down the hill she spotted
A camel caravan.

Holly Berry's prince
The rascal son of the King
(Who married a Popsicle
but you remember that story),

Anyway, there the Prince sits
What a sight he emits
Atop the lead camel
With flags blaring and trumpets flying.

A few meters back
With his guards on track
Comes the King whose son married
You know who
A day he may rue
If the saying be true
"Hell hath no fury like a monarch scorned."

With the Queen on a goat... needless to say
The King's fate remote... at least for that day.

She could do nothing but glare
At the camel's clip clop
And watch as they passed her by.

Her disguise in tact
She followed the pack

'Till the width of her mount caused her pain
She wouldn't try that again.

XV.

When the dogs are fed
And she goes to bed
She dreams of Pondicherry
Not the King of Holly Berry
(As one would suspect.)

India might send a suitor
In the guise of a tutor
Who knows? She could dream
So at least.

She dripped ten drops of calea
Under her tongue one night
So when her head nods
She calls in sleep gods

She found Indians more glamorous
Certainly more amorous
Than any she'd known so far.

In the land of the Ganges
In spite of the sand fleas
She walks on the shore
And buys far more
Than her courtier can carry

Sigh, just a dream
She'll soon awaken
To feed the dogs
And slop the hogs.

It's an early rise
One might surmise

Especially for a Queen.

XVI.

When she's happy
She saves jars
And writes letters.

No one ever looks
Not even the cooks.
The jars are covered with rugs.

Things hum around the palace
Time stands still
(They forgot to refill
The hourglass jugs.)

Any Queen who is keen
To slop hogs
Feed dogs and save jars
is a riddle to be sure
There is no cure for such.

Unless, of course, she sinks
Into worry and thinks… Then
There would be hell to pay every day.
Insoluble problems
Loomed large on the hill
More money may help
So she stuffed the till.

(The Queen can mint new green.)

She'll drag the jars
From under the rugs
And toss them pell-mell come Tuesday.

Letters? What ho.
They have to go,
For it's back to the status quo.

Her fun now gone
She looks a bit wan.

But her subjects are fine
Toasting with wine
The ways of the old
The way they've been told.

(The Queen doesn't care.
She'll just do her hair
And sit on her Ermine throne.)

XVII.

She loves to read
String an occasional bead
While swinging in her hammock chair.

Her thoughts aloft
The music too soft
To notice a big brown bear.

He sniffed at her brow
And gave her a bow
His fowl breath disagreeably near.

She wakened to find
That he didn't mind
Gladdened to show her his rear.

As he skipped past the gate
Left open of late,
Much to the Queen's dismay,

She didn't feel bad
Just a little bit sad
When the brown bear sauntered away.

XVIII.

The Queen doesn't fly
Yet high in the sky
She finds herself looking down.

"Planes are so tacky
You'd have to be wacky
To submit to it like a clown."

"I'm almost ready"
She called to her steady
As she packed for their midnight flight

"It's astral, you know," said he,
As she soared over the tree
And they didn't come back all night.

XIX.

Her plans were perfection
But she missed her connection
The plane was delayed at the gate.

Hours later she found
Feet hitting the ground
Forty-five minutes too late.

The Queen rarely flies
It's her monarchical ties
That keeps her riding the train.

Her travels are fewer
To fly not a lure
In her majesty's current reign.

They will want to approach
For the Queen is wearing her gaudy brooch.

Its glitter and swank
Will surely outrank
All the others.

When you know how to dazzle
In anyone's castle
You'll always be sought to join
The elite of the state
In the halls of the great

To sit by the Ruler and Prince
Whom she didn't have to convince
That Nappy's way with lawn croquet
Was the Queen's greatest pleasure.

Croquet was a sport of regal deport
Not of the masses
But played widely on grasses
Of bloodlines accustomed to leisure.

Nappy would get up every morn
And be seen on the green in his jammies

The keepers did wake
And leap out of sleep
To take care of
Grandfather Nappy.

They kept the mallets and balls and wickets
In a safe place overnight,
Lest Nappy might
Appear in the dark and just for a lark
Play on the lawn until almost dawn.

He could scarcely be scolded
Nappy much too olded for that.
What was it worth
To see such mirth
On the face the likes of his?

The Queen wasn't about
To tell what she'd found
Or bandy about his secret.

If the Emperor knows
That's how it goes
He enjoys no audience to mention.

The Prince may tell
But what the hell
A bellicose youth without any couth
Gets precious little attention.

The Queen left the great ball
Her gaudy brooch and all

Out the gate was she
Home too late too see

If Nappy was up
With his croquet tee
Out on the moonlit green.

XXI.

The Queen wants to go
Can't wait to sow
Her seeds of love and laughter.

(The Conference Works)

This doer of good
Soon out in the hood
Will ever after
Shout to the rafter
The lessons taught.

Her consciousness raised
She'll tell the others
If she has her druthers
That love is all there is.

Back at the castle
She succumbs to the hassle.
Finding it weird
This new way not geared
To the mundane life of the people.

She'll ring the bell
And set out to tell
The good news – Godspell.

In one ear straight across and out the other
Not fertile ground
Where thoughts can stand
And flag down a brother.

Awe heck, she's a wreck until
They toss the steak upon the grill

And she goes back to where she started
Before trying to incur
A new way to see
Like a bee attracted only to nectar.

XXII.

One day she was walking
And talking
And talking and walking
Almost missing it.

Ah, there it was
Just what she was searching for

A framed picture of trees
By a painter who pleased.

What happened next?
A bargaining scene
(Not to demean
Her highness, the Queen)
The purchase was cheap

The painting a print, a facsimile tint
"No one will know it
I'll just stow it.

Then, when I reveal
It will look quite real
To my subjects at large
Who are always in charge

Of my reputation," reasoned the Queen.

XXIII.

She was circumscribed socially
In a box like a fox.

She tried to extricate
And join the current debate

About a wandering war
More to deplore than fight.

Her people agreed
There was no need to escalate
But those in her court
At the tippy top top
Thought otherwise.

And set out to devise
A plan of action
With no retraction

Simply no way out.

It was forward into battle
(Just like the old hymn said)
Until you and you are dead

Sung in marching rhythm
Mighty warriors driven
By the charging call.

Heroes all or maybe not
Just hapless victims

Of an ill timed stance
A rivalry dance
For oil.

The Queen does not condone
Such carnage from her throne.

She falls far short
And would abort
The song this world is singing.

The ageless lore
That war is more
And worth the cost
Of millions lost

But this must CHANGE.

XXIV.

Her hair is white
You have no right to doubt her
Her majesty, the Queen.

But her hair was silly
Her blouse too frilly
The General kept his distance

Slipping just past, for instance,
the polished dance floor

Where her grace had placed
Her kerchief of lace
To entice a paramour

The commander of all who came
Of all but me, thought she
She, who could have crowned him King.

Her plans fell through
As plans often do.

It seems this mighty general thought
That battles fought
(Even with your Queen)

Could best be won
With half a ton of green
(And he didn't mean... celery).

And that was out
This white haired Queen had seen
Just too many wars.

XXV.

She's at the helm
The Queen of the realm

Her keel lies deep
In the cold and murky sea

Her rudder strong
Torqued by her majesty.

The waves can lap
She'll e'en take her nap
When the occasion arises.

There are no prizes
Nor lively surprises
For keeping awake
For heaven's sake
Let her sleep

In dreams she'll remember
A chill December

When his majesty left on a gurney
His last journey of this life.

He's gone now we know
But there's still a glow

Where' ere in thought he appears
Yet, there'll always be tears.

Her mascara runs and muddies her face.
Even the snails don't want to race
And rhyming this couplet
Is beyond her grace.

Then as if by magic
Though his leaving tragic

She finds reward
In waking toward

The Sun, the giver of life.

XXVI.

She wanted to sing
But it wasn't her thing

It seems when she tried
The audience sighed

Applause was polite
Who would deign to slight

Her highness, the Queen?

She made a stab at acting.
It wasn't so exacting.

Off key she could be
All would agree.

The Queen looked fine
Without even a sign

Of stage fright.
Why she just might

Make it on stage
Were she to engage in the theatre.

XXVII.

But what really makes her whole
Her passion for paint

Revealing the saint without constraint
Deep within her soul

Colors seduce her
And brushes reduce her
To a slave of canvas and art

The Queen can't wait to start
Doing her teensy part

Proclaiming to all
The creative muse
Reduces the blues

Easily besting the mall.

XXVIII.

"Queen's dance, too," she said
As they led her off the stage

Her friends at court, a helpful sort,
Included her favorite page,

Who heard as she left, applause,
Which gave him pause
To consider that, after all,
She *was the queen.*

And could do as she wanted
As she twirled and vaunted

Her royal position
There would be no revision

As long as she was seen
To be the queen in charge.
Dancing at large on every barge
Within the city limit.

She could join and thus purloin
The votes of those
Who would propose

To stop this silly practice
Of dancing long and with a song
Dispelling signs of malice.

Alas, she won – the deed is done
And war no more abounds.

Just check the empty arsenal or the street
And everywhere you go you'll meet
A curtsy and a smile.

Nothing to challenge the air of grace
That pervades the glades
Of this happy place.

That's all (for now)

About The Author

(Thought I'd just try it on for size)

Dorothy Baker is an artist and writer who makes her home in Yucca Valley, California, which may be the unsailed sea she speaks about in her memoir, *Picking Up Gum Wrappers & Everyday Magic*. Dorothy's adventures takes the reader from Studio City, CA, to Medfield, MA, to Sedona, AZ, to Mountainair, NM to New York City to be with her daughter who was married to a writer. It was there in the city that she began to write her memoir and the verses that became this little book, *The Queen*.

travelingshoespress.com/thequeen

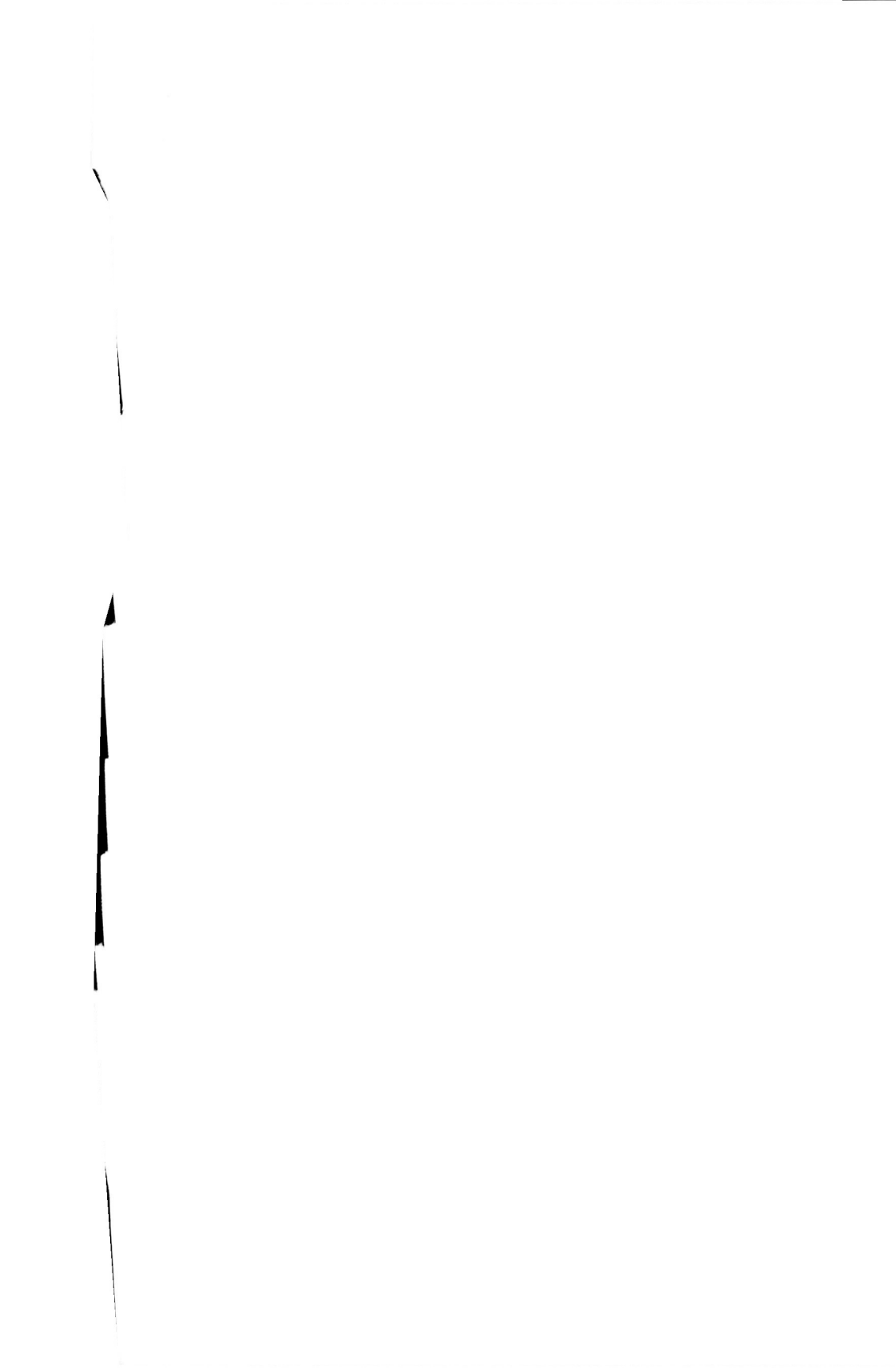

www.ingramcontent.com/pod-product-compliance
Lightning Source LLC
Chambersburg PA
CBHW051045030426

42339CB00006B/213